Growing Through Grief
A Poet's Journey From Pain To Peace

TEAIRHA L WASHINGTON

Growing Through Grief: A Poet's Journey From Pain To Peace

Copyright © 2015 Teairha L Washington

All rights reserved. No part of this publication may be reproduced, distributed or transmitted in any form or by any means including photocopying, recording or electronically or otherwise without written authorization from the publisher, except in cases of brief quotation within critical reviews and other noncommercial uses permitted by copyright law.

ISBN: 0692575995
ISBN-13: 978-0692575994

DEDICATION

I dedicate this book to my Dad. After all, Dad was the first man I ever loved. He worked hard and invested his confidence, his own limitless potential and seeds of encouragement in me. He never questioned my ability to do anything. Where I nursed my own doubts, hindering my own progress, my father was ever proud and always assured me that I was smart and able to pursue anything I wanted, to whatever ends I desired. It has taken me over 30 years to put his faith into action, by first developing my own and leaping head first, into what fits me like a magic glove. My poetry. I only wish I would have acted while he was still alive to witness my leap of faith, himself.

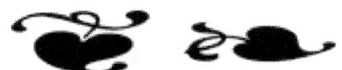

I dedicate this book to you. To whomever this bout with life has left with a proverbial scar. Someone for whom the depths of grief has shackled itself to, the sadness no one knows. The tears you cry in the dark when no one's watching. Navigating the wilderness of sadness can be quite treacherous. There seems to be almost no warning when a fog of memory surfaces on the horizon, its looming alone sends you to the brink of tears. Even in the most crowded of spaces, no one sees the sun set around you and the moon hiding in the clouds when you find yourself in these dark places. These are the times when no one can keep you from your depression, because it can be a comfortable place to live for a while. I think of myself as having embarked on a journey in constant exodus overcoming the loss of my father. There are glimpses of light along the path. But many times they are fleeting. In the end, I guess it's up to us to notice that there is still something beautiful in frailty. There is still something to learn in all of life's teachable moments. I'm glad we're not alone. This is your journey, take all the time you need.

If your organization would like to contact Teairha L Washington for engagement, please email all interest requests to teairhawashington@ymail.com.

CONTENTS

Acknowledgments

From Darkness: Exploring Sadness, Bitterness and Anger

We Never Thought You'd Leave Us

The Tantrum I'm Too Old To Have

Who Will Show Me How To Push?

To Light: Remembering Love, Choosing Peace, and Honoring Memories

You Must Keep Living

Last Hope

What Is.

Measurable Growth

To Dad, With Love

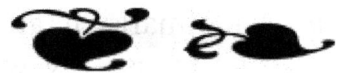

ACKNOWLEDGMENTS

I am eternally grateful to the creative energy (or God) that bestowed the gift of writing to me. Whatever the title, I know that I am not self-made, and I am still learning how to listen and trust the god energy within myself, to heal, learn and grow from. I am very thankful for each step of that process.

I would like to sincerely thank my parents, Michael Blick and Sandra McCoy. As the two of you have stood beside me in this calling and trusting its truth even more than I did. As I write this, I am reminded of reading my first "real poem" at my grandmother's funeral, after receiving it divinely and sharing it with my mourning family. Having both of you on either side cemented its importance and was a hallmark of all things poetic to later come. I will strive to use my work to make you both proud.

For my grandmothers, Sallie and Elsie,—who lived in such close proximity in both community and in spirit, I find traces of both of you in me. The legacy of righteousness and feminine strength is one that I still stand in awe of, trying to understand. I am so proud to represent you. Thank you doesn't even begin to express my reverence for you.

I need to express a debt of gratitude for the love and consistency of my husband and best friend, Chris. To look back over life's road and our time together, I know, that one of the best blessings I have ever received has come to me in the form of you. You keep me grounded while giving me enough room to dance with my feet off of the ground sometimes. Thank you for being all I could have ever hoped for in a husband, friend and companion in life. From helping me to care for my dying father, to the proper raising of our children, your compassion and unique view of any circumstance is why I always seek your advice and support. To the little people we've created, our children, Christopher, Kalei and Kaiyn-- Mommy needs to thank you too. Thank you for inspiring me with your endless faith. I always strive to encourage you to be positive and never give up because that's what you do for me. Thank you for helping me to mirror the law of attraction. I would like to specifically acknowledge the support of one of my favorite organizations, Heal A Woman to Heal A Nation and founders Mothyna James-Brightful and Monokia Nance; were it not for the constant support and demand for accountability, this work might still be in a folder on my desk. And for my dear sister-friend, the answer to a shared prayer, Tamyamonic Clowney, thank you for pushing me, and showing me that it can be done, sharing your spotlight and encouraging me to live with my readers in mind.

Thank you to Michael McCoy and Rose Gamble, for enduring many long winded conversations about every detail of the process of seeing this book to completion.

To Christine and Denise, where ever I am, I take you with me. Let's get it! To the vendors, resources and service providers who stand shoulder to shoulder with me, who supported this mission and signed on with me from the beginning, in an effort to heal humanity, I am eternally grateful. Thank you and I assure you, that anyone you have ever offered a kind word to while grieving has never forgotten your heartfelt consideration.

From Darkness:

Exploring Sadness, Bitterness and Anger

"The empty, initial sense of disbelief..."

"Feeling the earth crumble beneath my feet..."

"I've lost all footing...all feeling. I am so utterly alone."

We Never Thought You'd Leave Us

We never thought you wouldn't survive
collective high spirits
speckled with moments of nail biting tension
and the frailty of uncertain-ness

We never thought you wouldn't make it
Until the lows of your illness unsettled us
rocked us right off of those theological high horses
and right into the empty bosom of another Christian colloquialism
...and I, your only daughter grew bitter and lonely
wishing I had a sister to give some of this pain to
Some of the responsibility of keeping you
willing to live

I remember the day you gave up
Puzzled and angry that there was nothing more coming
a stroke
spilling yourself across my kitchen floor
Certainly, not the strong, silent type of man I admired
and came to for comfort
and my eyes are sore from crying grief tears
and I thought I had closed such a sad chapter
wondering when I'll be happy to make you proud
feeling more like a brat whose spoiled fits of tantrum
never really....get me anywhere

I'm defeated and disappointed to learn
that I haven't figured out how to deal with this yet

TEAIRHA L WASHINGTON

" When I can't stop crying... "

"When I can't sleep, think or even take my next breath... "

"I just need to hear your voice...and I can't... "

The Tantrum I'm Too Old To Have

Today I am fragile
and no amount of coddling gives me strength
I don't wanna get outta bed
So let me wallow in the misery
That I call Life Void

Ironically....
I feel like we can be alone here
and in this space
I can have you to myself
Let me cry out loud enough
maybe I'll interrupt heaven
Long enough to hear from you
The turbulence in my mind is overwhelming
and I need a reality break

So I'm going to wail, to moan
I'm going to whine and question God
rebelling against his choice to separate us

And SCREAM out loud
because
I'm hurting
broken
I don't like pain

And I can't
...fix this

TEAIRHA L WASHINGTON

Growing Through Grief: A Poet's Journey From Pain To Peace

I can't undo this
couldn't stop this
and in this moment
It's too much
And I'm entitled to a tantrum
every once in a while

Cuz you'd holler too
If you loved like I loved
and lost like I lost
feel peril and pain
when time is not long enough
and eternity is forever

I miss running in the rain with you
like when we were children
and make memories that never happened

I'm stuck

cuz I can't

and all I have is this paper
So I'll collect my disappointment
funnel it into a waterfall and bathe in my sadness
and I'll be done, when I'm done
and when I'm done
I'll be clean

TEAIRHA L WASHINGTON

"How long will I feel this way?"

"I don't know how to move forward, I'm not even sure I want to."

"I saw someone who reminded me of you today...and for a moment I forgot that you were gone."

Growing Through Grief: A Poet's Journey From Pain To Peace

Who Will Show Me How To Push?

Who will teach me how
To walk through life without you
To carefully pick up the pieces
And put myself together again

Who will teach me how
Not to squander the time I have here
To instead be resilient and steadfast
Finding joy
While pursuing my own personal greatness

Who will frame the losses of my life
With sunny smiles, wry humor, and the gentleness
You quietly pocketed when you left

And when I'm looking for inspiration
Who will teach me how to look within
Peering past the fogginess of melancholy
for traces of your smile emblazoned over a sunny horizon

Some sign that the outpouring of tears
A humble gesture, my offering to God
In exchange for the tranquility of comfort
In manifesting peace

Take heart, dear loved ones

TEAIRHA L WASHINGTON

Our journey together continues
despite your change in formation

We are stronger than we look
and than we feel
As this moment
is but one star, in the expanse of the universe
fleeting courage

This moment
is but one ripple
in an ocean of many tides

You
You are loved....
And not forgotten

For this reason, our progression continues
Ever knowing
that you are standing, lovingly and in respected authority
as a teacher
showing us the way

TEAIRHA L WASHINGTON

To Light:

Remembering Love, Choosing Peace and Honoring Memories

TEAIRHA L WASHINGTON

"Everyone keeps telling me that it's time for me to move on. You wouldn't want to see me to living like this... and in my heart of hearts, I know they're right."

"My family needs me today."

You Must Keep Living

Greatness comes
with the stamina of unfettered determination
Outlasting excuses
and often on the heels of sufferance and disappointment

Renewal and knowingness
That survival is not a choice
But simply, the only option

As much as we smile
head nodding, phony lips curled into a lie of pleasantry

We are broken
and repaired
Tied to one another
anchored in elasticity
Vibrantly renewed some days
Sluggish and unable to continue others

Our losses mirrored in the pain of sorrowful
remembrances
and the bubbles of laughter
that marks todays distraction
An unrelenting cycle
of grief and personal mediocrity
A hamster wheel of progress and despair
Purely tactic of survival
because no one really knows how it feels

to bury a child,

TEAIRHA L WASHINGTON

a mother,
a father
brother
or dearest friend
and at some point
everybody else limps forward
moving on
barely glancing backward
expecting you to
too

Revive yourself
breathing in waves of breaths
of waiting peace
wrap yourself in the cloaking comfort
settling into adversity
into the stretching of your own spirit
fortifying you
making you whole
making you love

again
knowing that an exercise in growth past this point
will be chiseled from your own relentlessly unbounded
will
providing just enough backbone
to stand tall
and free another on the brink
After all,
the linking of humanity lies

in the humility of loss and collective devastation

TEAIRHA L WASHINGTON

*"I wonder where you are and if you're happy...
...or what you'd say to me if we had one more chance to speak..."*

Last Hope

Endure me no longer as I sing my thoughtless tune
Why buy a flower if its dead and cannot bloom?
Think not of me, beyond the grave
Think not of the attention I do not crave

Too much confusion
a decision too large
I can't make by myself
Why put me in charge?

Listen to the song of the sweet nightingale
Moans of hungry children
So helpless and frail

Doubt not my abilities
I have faith to wander on
Doubt not my actions
For I need no shoulder to cry upon

So dry thine eyes
Wipe away those scars of pain
Life for me, ain't over yet
For I got too much to gain

TEAIRHA L WASHINGTON

"Sometimes I find myself willing me to move on, maybe that's how I'll get through this..."

"I'm grateful today."

"...grabbing my own hand and pulling myself forward"

What Is

A heavily condensated breath
full of warmth
pain
catharsis
acceptance
and a reminder
That it is time to let go

It is what it is

Finality and confirmation
lends itself
acceptance comes in many forms
raw and obvious
honest and slow
Knowing that should bring about
fruitful understanding

It's time to pick up heavy feet and keep moving
Catch up with life and the living
To question what is
wastes time
and its it's own answer

Lightness of mind is an enjoyable quality
If you can allow yourself
To accept
What Is

TEAIRHA L WASHINGTON

Growing Through Grief: A Poet's Journey From Pain To Peace

You don't have to like what is
Understand that what is
doesn't need your permission or approval
to be

Sit yourself in the stillness of what is
Letting your own breath relieve you

Mind mantras replay themselves
Crashing against the walls of your mind
like heavy, solid waves
sturdy and cleansing
Battering brain boulder burdens
Over time
softening the stone
smoothing stubborn sharpness
ebbing edges
with the tide of time

What is?
What is.
What. Just. Is.
Stop asking
And clench peace

TEAIRHA L WASHINGTON

"I think you'd be proud of me."

*"I've learned how to make peace with your transition.
...because love transends all of time, and all of everything else too."*

Measurable Growth

In the space of exploration of love
pleasing to the minds eye
I see us together
holding hands
eyes smiling and watery
as I recognize missing you
loving you
and every tearfully progressive step of this journey
learning to comfort myself in your absence

You were my favorite
And even in trying to prepare myself for your transition

I found myself...
perilously unprepared

And yet...
I can close my eyes and see your happy face
cheerfully
the way we remember
and hear laughter in the rustle of leaves
basking in the warmth of the sunshiny twinkle in your eyes

Amazed and astonishingly
bathed in the blessing
that even in your absence
You're still giving me beautiful memories

TEAIRHA L WASHINGTON

I am revitalized, radiant and reborn
New and magnificent
As celebratory thoughts flood heartfelt memories
a gentle misted rain
Sings from the corners of my eyes

You dance on the riverbed of my heart
Arms outstretched
Triumphantly
delighted

TEAIRHA L WASHINGTON

*"For stepping into my life for a brief period, and changing me forever...
for gracefully molding me into a more compassionate and humane individual...
for a great many other contributions, too numerous to name,*

...thank you."

To Dad, With Love

I let you go Dad
Releasing all the memories I've been holding
in balled fists
for the sake of...
your presence

I let you go
so that I can live
happy and smiling

I let you go
because I want to run past the borders
of disappointing hopefulness
and being let down every morning rise
to the angry reality
that you're still gone, and I'm still here
without you

Somewhere you knew I'd struggle

and I appreciate the honor in your vigilance
and resolve to win
a fixed fight

So you stayed a while longer
borrowing a few extra days
from a Creator that needed to prepare you
prepare me

TEAIRHA L WASHINGTON

for the next assignment

So I'll let you go
and fill the remaining emptiness
with excitement
passion
anticipation and love

I've released your spirit
and embraced mine

A LETTER TO MY READERS

I am writing this letter to the person who is broken hearted and feeling utterly devastated by the loss of a loved one. I know that this part of a book is usually reserved for an *About the Author* section, but I'd rather offer a bit of heartfelt commentary instead.

Firstly, I want to say that if you are holding this book, and felt the ominous pain of loss, I want to tell you that I understand. I wrote this book after I lost my father to lung cancer. My husband and I moved him into our home and cared for him from the day that he was diagnosed, until the day he passed away. I watched him every day. Initially, as the strongest man I ever knew and finally, as a broken spirited, fragile and unfamiliar father succumbing to a wretched, and catastrophically terrible disease.

Near the end, I was able to lovingly cradle him as he made peace with his fate. With the help of a beautiful team of humane nurses, my family and I eased him as lovingly as we could into a tranquil state at home, fulfilling his final request. Throughout this process I grieved the idea of losing him. I spent many nights in his bedroom, talking until he fell asleep or until I had no more words left.

I felt all sorts of emotions initially. I remember getting a call from my husband on the morning Dad passed. I knew from his tone that he was calling to say that Dad was gone. During the last three days of his life,

I'd asked my husband to give my father his morning dose of Morphine, as I did not want to be the one to discover that he had passed. I set to work in other ways, mentally finalizing arrangements and calling extended family members and being the stoic rock that everyone else needed. I remember getting lost on the way home from work that day. A route I'd previously taken for years, became questionably perplexing on the day Dad died. My mind was on auto-pilot. There was a non-stop overflow of people in and out of the house that day. From medics and professional people to family members we hadn't seen in months all coming to gather together and pay their respects.

I remember the annoyance I felt by their sudden presence, and thought of how much my husband and children had been through getting Dad to countless chemotherapy sessions and doctor's appointments. I wondered where they had been when Dad was still alive and needed them. It wasn't until about a month later that I learned how to think of their efforts in a new perspective.

I learned that death is probably the most uncomfortable aspect of life. And more importantly, that my annoyance was displaced. I had, without permission taken on the emotions of my father, and that wondering about the significance of my father in their lives was none of my business. I decided to instead focus on practicing tolerance, and to meet people where they are. It's not my job to police anyone's relationship or love for my father. I'd done all that I felt I could do for him, and that's all that mattered. I learned that after one conversation with my husband. And after putting it to practice, I gave myself the gift of peace, and focused on having good relationships with all of my relatives.

The gift that I received after I let go of being annoyed with some of them manifested itself in the form of learning how my father had impacted their lives. It's one thing to know "Dad" as his first born daughter: a strict guy, the quiet disciplinarian, the first man to have ever successfully been tied around my baby finger. But it's an altogether different experience to hear stories about dad as the cool uncle, or rebellious youth. Stories that he'd never tell about himself. Hidden in those stories are the gems that allowed my dad to live despite dying. I craved those stories and everyone who'd ever loved him had them and shared them freely. It's been so easy for them to get lost in sharing the details of a good memory once they start talking. I am so glad I'm not still walking around with the negative energy of that annoyance.

After he passed, I thought that I'd come through the hardest part of losing him. It wasn't until exactly five months after he passed, the exact five months from diagnosis to death, when I woke up screaming in the middle of the night, that it truly hit me that he was gone, and that the hardest part of my life had just begun.

I won't tell you how to grieve. Or how long it will be before the nightmare of loss is over for you. What I can tell you, is that there is a life waiting for you after you're finished. My grieving process ended with the completion of this book. My father passed away four years ago. That was my timeline.

I decided to channel the pain of losing my father into helping other grief survivors to heal and to share their stories. Since I've turned this path in my journey, I've held hands and cried with people I never knew my story would ever touch. I realized how spoiled and unappreciative I've been to sulk in misery, angry for losing Dad so soon when I've had my father on this earthly plane for a lifetime compared to the children I shared my story with whose parents have transitioned. I remember when I figured that I'd try to help and encourage them, and knew later that their strength and resolve to move forward was what fortified me to continue. Oh, the irony of this journey!

I believe that we are all a part of something bigger, and that there is some gift that we owe to humanity to share. Your life has a purpose. And it's so much bigger than being curled up in bed, in a state of emotional wreck. That's a part of the process, believe me. But it doesn't end there. You owe it to the memory of your loved one, to finish your story, purposefully. Give that gift to humanity that is within you to give. And do it with your loved one in mind. It really is the only way to pay homage to the beautiful human experience that this person has shared with you. It's the making of your very own legacy. I encourage you that when you are ready, to please consider exploring it. We need it, and we need you.

Your Sister,

Growing Through Grief: A Poet's Journey From Pain To Peace

*For Elsie,
Melvin,
Shirley,
Richard,
Sheila,
Neil,
Lamont,
James,
Faybienne and*

....Dad

Growing Through Grief: A Poet's Journey From Pain To Peace

www.ingramcontent.com/pod-product-compliance
Lightning Source LLC
Chambersburg PA
CBHW051712090426
42736CB00013B/2673